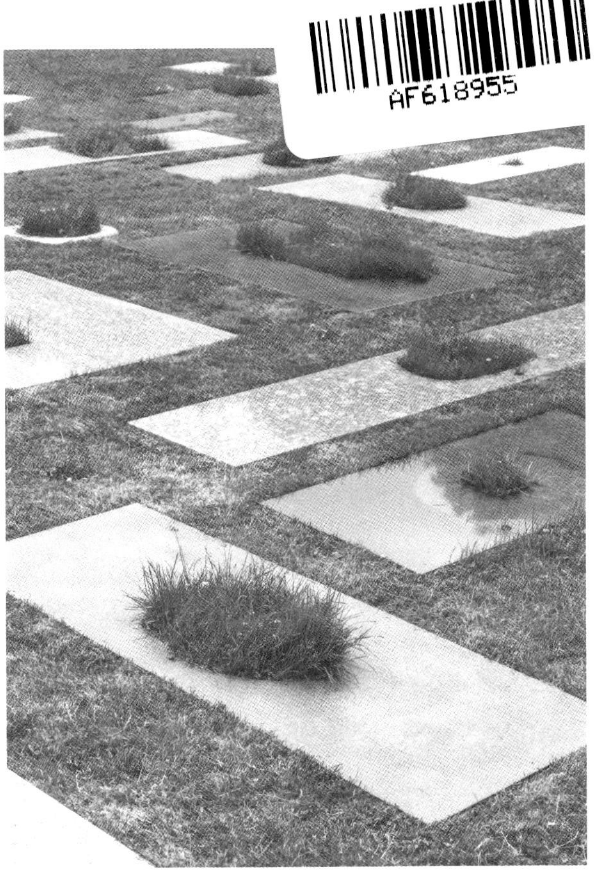

Nina Beier, *Ø (Island)*, 2024

COMMODITY ECUMENE: ON THE ART OF NINA BEIER

JEPPE UGELVIG

Gl. Holtegaard Bierke Verlag

It's hard to look at a product and perceive its total reality. The meanings of the commodity—its origins, its uses, its values—lie stacked within it as sediments, layered knowledges in fractured form. A discarded pinkish marble countertop, for example, always comes from somewhere. Before it reached the gardens of Gammel Holtegaard art center just north of Copenhagen, as part of the artwork *Island* (2024) by the artist Nina Beier, it was purchased and used by someone who, for some reason, identified with it, found it meaningful enough to buy and coexist with and look at, at least for a period of time. Of course, before that, the countertop was manufactured—extracted from the earth's carbonate bedrock, cut and polished into a recognizable shape by laboring hands. It was packaged, shipped, displayed, marketed—socialized into a wider consumer trend across great distances—into a semantic network of mediated images in which marble surfaces and countertops figured as fashionable. Before installation, it was customized to fit sinks, faucets, and other features as per the buyer's specific needs, leaving irreversible incisions on its hard body. No doubt did this lapidarian stamp, annulling countless potential refittings, contribute to its eventual discarding—like a puzzle piece that refuses to fit. Marked by time and a particular context, it was difficult for this once-dazzling commodity to regain its former raison d'être—and by extension, its former exchange value. Yet, somehow, this countertop has found a new purpose in a new arena, that of contemporary art. As part of *Island*, it lies flat on a lawn alongside dozens of variably perforated stone countertops of a very similar type. They are components of an artwork, though lying there, scattered around the lawn with little pretext, they may more closely resemble gravestones, ancient artifacts slowly becoming one with their environment. Like the surrounding baroque gardens, the lawn is pristinely manicured, except for the bits growing buoyantly from the stone's perforations. The gardener has been instructed to leave them to grow until the exhibition's run sometime in the winter. They look like crazy haircuts or beards. Of course, they are still countertops, somehow. It is raining.

It is hard to look at a product and perceive its total reality, but Beier invites us to, seductively—however personal, contradictory, or inadequate our perception may be. The great mystic of commodity culture, Roland Barthes, was right to point out that man-made objects are tricky semantic vehicles because they persist in existing "somewhat against us": a thing is never reducible to its function and, rather, there is "always a meaning which overflows the object's use."[1] These resistant meanings are not easily decipherable, for things are not mere utilities to a world in action but participants and agents in it. To trade epistemologically in the world of things is to trade in the dialectics of, on the one end, the banal or overfamiliar, and, on the other, the profoundly unknowable. Beier's art exists there, in that tense in-between, searching for the product's ability to speak, to be, somehow, *meaningful*.

1
Roland Barthes, *The Semiotic Challenge* (University of California Press, 1984), 184–89.

Barthes's theory of semiotics drew on the anthropologist and linguist Claude Lévi-Strauss, who once mused that the human labor of bricolage—the creative putting-together of things—"is itself the seeking-out and the imposition of a meaning upon the object."[2] In order to find absolutely improvised—that is to say meaningless—objects or object formations, we should have to proceed to completely asocial states. No doubt would both Barthes and Lévi-Strauss have chuckled at Beier's sensuous sculptural evidence of such semantic hyperactivity, of the object's "refusal to be tamed," as the artist herself has quipped in relation to another project of hers about marble, *Guardian* (2021). The work explicates a different but similarly ubiquitous product, "guardian lions," typically found as ornamental sculptures by the entrances of homes, palaces, tombs, or places of worship. Historically, such lions are surprisingly transcultural objects, traceable to as early as Ancient Greece, India, and China, and share a symbolic function: to mark the threshold between inside and outside, between public and private property, which the lion, as the proverbial "king of beasts," is purported to protect. Of course, the lion keeping guard is an absurd symbol if you really think of it, considering that lions cannot actually be tamed; as such, these statues more accurately represent the enduring human illusion of dominance over nature. Today, most marble lions are mass-produced in China and sent all over the world from there. For the work *Guardian*, Beier amassed two dozen or so and installed them in an old barn at Rønnebæksholm kunsthal, displaying them on their sides as if tumbled over. To accompany these fallen guardians — their authority symbolically annulled — Beier let the local cats roam the barn, lapping a range of commercial milk (cow, almond, and "cat-friendly") from crevices in the stone lions' undulating surfaces.

Marble (a metamorphic carbonite rock formation) has been caught in commodity trend cycles since its earliest human extraction more than 2,000 years ago. In the process, it has aggregated social and cultural meanings and forms of value, absorbing some of the intentions with which it was made — how it was valued and, by extension, traded (the same goes for real lions, by the way: lions aren't native to China, but history suggests that a handful had arrived from the West

2
Claude Lévi-Strauss, *The Savage Mind* (University of Chicago Press, 1969), 2.

around 100 BCE as gifts and commodities and were since kept in the imperial parks of the Han Dynasty for spectacle and enjoyment). Surely, many of these meanings were lost in the process, too—just as some leave traces and are subject to sudden retrieval. By the new millennium, marble had taken on a rather garish and outmoded connotation in the realm of interior decorating, no doubt aided by its plain impracticality (a notoriously porous stone, marble cleans poorly), but it has recently made a triumphant return in homes and hotels around the world, recontextualized to connote a new global aesthetic of unabashed luxury. Effectively, the extraction of marble continues: when The Venetian Resort in Las Vegas needed large swaths of marble for its recent $1.5 billion renovation, they proceeded with buying an entire mine of it in Italy for the purpose. Vast geological, human, technological, and economic forces were at work for millennia before gambling shoppers could peruse the air-conditioned, marble-clad boulevards deep in the Nevada desert, an environment that feels so environmentally fictitious that the *real* Italian marble there could easily be mistaken for—well, being *fake*. For marble, like many materials used by human culture, doubles as a semiotic signified, that is to say, *as image*. And such images are themselves often rematerialized, for example, as a textured pattern in ceramic and vinyl flooring. This leads to yet another work by Beier, *Tileables* (2016), where the artist installed a floor of various commercial ceramic tiles printed with images of clay, marble, and other natural surfaces. These could be dismissed as fake tiles until you realize that they are, in fact, *both* real tiles and *images* of real tiles. By stepping on the tiles, as Beier invites us to, one treads directly on a foundation between object and representation, where the image is subsumed into the object and the other way around. The rapaciousness of the digital image, its technologies of production and reproduction, is activated only to support our ideas of the slowest, most aged of matter—stone.

All of this, somehow, loops back to *Island*, to the gardens of Gammel Holtegaard, where it is still raining. As an installation of found objects, it offers a wealth of entry points for the viewer and welcomes them all equally: one might ponder the millennia-long formation period of carbonite rock made commodity only to now be returned symbolically to the soil. Another might be reminded of trendy bachelor pads of the 1980s, or differently, the rise of "kitchen islands" in the same decade, when the

Western kitchen found a new purpose as an arena of leisure and social reproduction in the midst of rapid lifestyle changes, probed by the ongoing rise of the modern nuclear family and the female workforce. A third will recall the marble sculptures of Ancient Greece or Rome, known for their sublime white polish, which was later symbolically coded as part of a European aesthetic and intellectual Renaissance—a visual culture that itself was symbolically *re*coded as ethnonationalist by Nazi Germany during the Second World War. This is despite the fact that these three-dimensional portraits in stone (it has since become emphatically clear) were rarely experienced as whitewashed in their own time, for they were most often painted in realistic skin tones (with pigment, alas, that has since faded, eroded along with its cultural ubiquity). Fans of contemporary art may think of the muted but insisting presence of minimalist sculpture and works of land art, such as Nancy Holt's unobtrusive concrete tubes in the empty Utah desert. And so on and so on. The key to Beier's work—where it truly reveals its critical capacities, its poetic depth, its joyful sense of humor—is its attempt to hold up these vectors of perception simultaneously, to move both vertically and horizontally in our analytic probing of the knowledges that things possess within them or the knowledges they remind us of in ourselves—knowledges about the wild symbolic and material movements of things within commodity capitalism, which include the realm of the linguistic as well as the semantic space of art. For *Island* and *Guardian*, of course, are Beier's own addition to the vast story of marble: if the first is a symbolic graveyard for past domestic typologies of domestic social reproduction, the latter becomes a cheeky monument to the full domestication of nature, where animal, earth, soil, and body are spectacularly extracted for value, be it as food, decor, or companionship.

Beier gathers commodities new and old, dead or alive, to produce what Walter Benjamin once called "dialectical images": a way of seeing "that crystallizes antithetical elements by providing the axis for their alignment."[3] The dialectical image shows us a synthetic view of history that is distinct for holding together inherently unreconciled elements, which resists an illusionistic and harmonic perception of the past. For Benjamin, whose main interest was

3
Susan Buck-Morss, *The Dialectics of Seeing: Walter Benjamin and the Arcades Project*, rev. ed. (MIT Press, 1991), 210.

the early consumer society of the nineteenth century, this axis of contradiction was found best in the commodity form, with its many "faces" — fetish, fossil, wish image, ruin — that appear to us as various intensities of legibility in its arrested, physical state. The philosopher's laboratory for this fickle concept was his *Arcades Project*, an ambitious (and unfinished) collection of writing fragments associatively compiled in portfolios under evocative categories such as "iron construction," "spa," "mirrors," and "modes of lighting."[4] Like Beier, Benjamin reached intuitively into the logics of cultural heritage, interior design, art, literature, urban planning, politics, and economy to find the deep historical knowledges latent in literal products — commodities, wares, purchasable goods — of capitalist modernity. Similarly, the result is imagistic and evocational rather than scientific or didactic, producing images of cultural realities that flicker poetically and ultimately rely on the reader's own imaginative participation and the meanings they bring to the object. If Benjamin's dialectic strategy was one of textual montage using the archive of the nineteenth century (itself an adaptation of surrealist visual technique), Beier's sculptural bricolage employs the symbolically charged frame of contemporary art, where we, as twenty-first-century museum-goers, are trained to consider all kinds of objects both thoroughly decontextualized and symbolically propped-up. Fitting objects into tightly curated environments that nonetheless feel entirely non-theatrical, Beier works seductively to "trigger" the immediately associative impulse as a way to test the extent of our — mine, yours, her own — cultural data set and the ability to retrieve it through the artwork.

SIGNS

Since Duchamp, we have gotten used to not entirely knowing what we look at in the art gallery and proceeding by following our proverbial gut — that is, our knowledge of symbolic forms, linguistics, and semiotics. Due to such knowledges, a signed urinal turned upside down and titled *Fountain* may become a titillatingly sexual innuendo to some and, to others, a blasphemic attack on the original skillfully executed work of fine art. A canvas of abstractly applied color splashes may symbolize the zero degree of the century-long Western

4
Walter Benjamin, *The Arcades Project* (Belknap Press, 1999).

painting tradition, or rather, signify the emotional interiority of its painter by way of vitalistic brushstrokes. In art, we always *look* but never without context; we are looking for *signs* to be symbolically decoded. Variations of this semiotic approach have long provided art history (and later, visual studies) a working methodology, informed by the earlier lessons of pictorial formalism and Panofskian iconology. Saussurean semiotics's structural division between the material signifier (a word, a sound, an image, an object) and a conceptual and presumably stable signified mediated by codes is at its heart linguistic: it implies local contexts of reading and modalities of legibility and illegibility. As an art-historical method, it inherently privileges the visual sign, the analysis of stable symbol orders perceptible and processable to a culturally trained eye.

Semiotics, as a study of symbols, is only secondarily connected to historical materialism. When the connection is pursued by semioticians, signs at best serve as neat symbolic representations of grand ideological formations such as "capitalism"; this is true for so-called social art history and even in the most ambitious readings of products, materials, and surfaces such as those presented in the late twentieth century by Barthes and Baudrillard—thinkers who proved that common children's toys are prefigurations of institutional bureaucracy and that pastels are false promises of nature offered by a technologized interior design industry.[5] Baudrillard, for one, wrote about marble during his infamous journey through the 1980s United States, characterizing it as promising a "minimalist extraterrestrial comfort," one of the "flawless, funereal" surfaces of Los Angeles and Salt Lake City, a place that "has the transparency and supernatural, otherworldly cleanness of a thing from outer space."[6]

If Beier's work fits nicely in such a methodology, it is only to exceed it. No doubt does she engage the realm of the semiotic: as curator Karen Archey once aptly phrased it, "Whether tactically filling up emptiness with loaded signifiers, or turning the emptiness itself into a loaded signifier, Nina Beier's work speaks to the complexities of a world that is pregnant with meaning."[7] Indeed, the punched-in

5
Roland Barthes, *Mythologies* (J. Cape, 1972) and Jean Baudrillard, *The System of Objects* (Verso, 1996).

6
Jean Baudrillard, *America* (Verso, 2010), 2.

7
Nina Beier, *Cash for Gold* (Mousse Publishing, 2017), 49.

countertops of *Island* look easily like signs of some lost, arcane alphabet. Their signifying potential is not one of linguistics as much as one of design morphology, each unique shape possessing its own set of sociocultural information (pertaining to taste and trend) in cryptic code—code legible to those familiar with it. But as explicated above, products (such as Beier's) carry information beyond the immediately visual and the broadly symbolic. In fact, Benjamin's historical materialism insisted that matter escapes signification, and by this, I don't mean as "empty" or "floating" signifiers (which temporarily suspends but nonetheless asserts the dualistic logic of the sign), but rather, that they *exceed* the realm of the sign: meanings *overflow* and *escape* at once. This "overflowing" is decisively materialist, that is to say, concerned with the movement of matter under capital—with vast networks of production, distribution, and exchange, to global political economies, which know no coherent language. These movements rarely guarantee stable representations and are frequently in contradictory relation to the symbolic order they nonetheless are partially subject to. They are meanings engendered by making, buying, using, selling, and throwing away. These are grounds for bewilderment but not despair, for we all have one tool or another ready to pick them apart—including, yes, the broadly symbolic. If Beier's art deepens the riddles of contemporary consumerism, it is because it confronts us with the joyful realization that we already *know so much*, so intimately, as a result of our participation and complicity.

DOGS AND COMMODITIES

The turning point for Beier came in the shape of a dead dog. It was at Kunsthal Charlottenborg in 2011 where a golden lab appeared to have taken its last breath atop a Persian rug right in the middle of the exhibition. For a few excruciating minutes, the dog—*taxidermized? Mummified?*—held a tight grip on its surroundings, fixating viewers in that uncanny valley between fatality and performance. But as the dog—which, in fact, was a canine actor hired by Beier to play dead—heard its trainer's cue amongst the crowd, got up, and proceeded to leave, leaving behind nothing but the rug (and a faint pile of dog hair), the visitors could sigh in relief, only to be left with a more complicated sensation: that tense oscillation between life, labor, and commodity.

Tragedy (2011) is a key work because it offers a physical experience of what representation is: the dog momentarily produces an image of itself as dead because of its charged institutional-semantic context (an art museum). This double identity, coexisting in a single, quivering moment in which an object appears as itself *and its representation*, runs through much of Beier's work, if only to highlight how this is rather common in our culture: a wig is a representation of human hair but *actually is* hair (see *Minutes*, 2013); an actor hired to cry is nevertheless *actually crying* (see *Drama*, 2019); a pressed and framed palm tree doubles as an image of itself (see *Greens*, 2013); and Beier's dog becomes an image—well, of what exactly? Of the absurdity of projecting our fear of death onto an animal, this spirited thing that we envy because it is not aware of its eventual death? Of the making-worker of our pets, destined for a life of entertainment?

Beier's work reminds us most vividly of anthropologist Arjun Appadurai's simple but so critical observation that "commodities represent very complex social forms and distributions of knowledge."[8] This is because the social, spatial, and temporal distances between producers and consumers in industrialized society, which crystalize no better than in the commodity form, are so vast that they escape a single semantic system and, thus, exceed any given standard analytical methodology. The problem with the "commodity" as a conceptual category—since Marx, defined as any object of exchange under capitalism—is found within its own historiography. Today, the category has come to span everything from the extraction of raw materials from the earth and petty trading in marketplaces to the selling of human labor, the circulation of mass-produced objects, the use of images for commercial purposes, and the various hybrid mutations between them. Conceptually, this is a far cry from Marx's episteme, writing as he did in the mid-nineteenth century in the midst of the initial commodification of human labor power by the industrializing capitalist economy, which he rightfully made his central theoretical problematic. But as many have since argued, Marx's productivist theory of wage labor is hardly an adequate theory for contemporary consumerism, not to mention for culturally embedded objects of exchange more generally,

8
Arjun Appadurai, ed., *The Social Life of Things: Commodities in Cultural Perspective* (Cambridge University Press, 1997), 41.

that have existed much longer than capitalist markets and which can potentially exist in any society insofar as a commodity can be *anything* intended for *any* kind of value exchange. Today, "commodity" spans things, artifacts, humans, futures; the concrete, the performative, the speculative, and the ephemeral. While this framework is not incorrect, it teaches us too little about the world of things.

Yet this messiness is exactly the purview of Beier, for not only do we humans subliminally and symbolically mix nature with the world of things, and humans with animals, so does capital. Let's return to the dog, which was hired by Beier by way of its owner, who was also hired by Beier. Thousands of dogs play dead every day as professional collaborators with their human owners, who themselves labor in performance economies of entertainment. Millions more dogs work in the realms of security, surveillance, farming, sports, and care. What's truly unfathomable, of course, is that dogs are themselves "man-made," living products of the thousand-year-long process of the domestication of wolves, not least via intricate selective breeding for the purposes of aesthetic and psychogenetic modification, which proliferated in Victorian England some two hundred years ago. Every dog somehow contains an entire history of commoditization, domination, control, manipulation, power, and design. And yet, it's just a dog.

Appadurai's edited volume *The Social Life of Things: Commodities in Cultural Perspective* (1986) stands as the most ambitious bid to reconceptualize our analytical approach to the commodity form. The proposal is simple enough: to attune us, through the lens of the anthropological, to an understanding of things as having cultural biographies and even "social lives." For if things – such as a marble countertop or dogs – change meaning, value, and function over the course of their existence, if they change hands and move around society, they are implicated in the social and in the political. Humans, of course, also often double as commodities, either as literal bodies (slavery, modeling, gestational surrogacy) or when providing services that are rendered valuable. Appadurai's motivation to propose the social life of things is not to animate them or give them agency of their own,[9] but rather, to more closely appreciate the intricate political economies in which they are embedded; that is, the human negotiation of value and power around and through things, also and especially when it is the human who is "thingified." One of the key interventions of Appadurai is an encouragement to think through the idioms of the social and the biographical, where "the commodity is not one kind of thing rather than another, but one phase in the life of something."[10] Rather than a stable identity for objects of certain significance within human society, commodity is best understood as the identity of something when it is, literally, "at market"—when something enters a situation of exchange, which always is the result of a "complex intersection of temporal, cultural, and social factors."[11] "Commodity" should not be seen as an ontologically stable state but, rather, a performatively liminal stage (Appadurai even at one point calls it a "career") in which value is asserted by a gathering of social players. Appadurai proposes a range of subcategories specifying the journey to and from such a stage: commodities "by destination," "by metamorphosis," "by diversion," and even "ex-commodities." The theory of the commodity may be a theory of embodied value but only insofar as it is a theory of "things-in-motion" driven by the socially performative vectors of value. Appadurai minces no words: "What creates the link between exchange and value is politics";[12] what constitutes a commodity is *always* a question of power.

Beier and Appadurai would be great co-conspirators, for Beier adds the symbolic lyricism of art to the philosopher's social science, which teases out the profound—and intensely—cultural information in objects. There is always too much meaning, as Barthes showed—the question is what we do with it. If we should stick to Appadurai's framework of the social, Beier's dialectics probes the messy "heritages" of things across matter and symbol, which are only perceptible as fragments in that they are highly contextual and ridden by obsolescence. Beier's work illuminates, animates, and illustrates such politics by illuminating the wild social lives of things: the way they journey through life stages, through cycles, periods, circuits of value, through image cultures, through human hands—all of which leave semantic residue deep within it. As such, Beier's art is

9
That would rather be New Materialism, a fascinating discourse that no doubt lies adjacent to Appaduarai's more traditional anthropological materialism. If Beier's work flirts with the suggestion of objects endowed with agency, it is to call upon various cultural symbolic orders that long have coexisted with exchange values within a commodity.

10
Appadurai, *The Social Life of Things*, 16.

11
Appadurai, 15.

12
Appadurai, 3.

an act of archeology, a game of probing and remembering the residual and almost forgotten.

ORIGINS

Over the last two decades, Beier has refined her ability to generate dialectical images through the commodity form. The journey to this methodology is itself salient, for it connects an almost exclusively object-based practice with a broader artistic strategy that perceives the world through multimedia repositories of "stuff" (commodities, images, discourses, histories), the proverbial "pile" of societal overproduction that can be sifted through by the artist in order to create a dialectics of life under capital. Beier (along with other artists of her generation, such as Henrike Naumann and Cameron Rowland) is only concerned with novel material production in art insofar as it can propose a critical discourse of re-circulation, and herein lies a critical ethic that thinks politically about value from all points in the chain or "life story" of things, including that of the artwork, the image, and the laboring human.[13]

While it is hardly visible today, Beier came up in the "post-internet" moment of art, a time of productive ontological inquiry into the digital image-as-commodity, which was still only in its earliest infancy of economization. Beier, then at art school in London, would spend her time perusing stock image banks, for they possess an attribute poignant to her interests: authorless and collectively produced, stock images are designed to symbolize the maximum amount of potential semantic meanings for markets unknown to their makers at the time of production. Stock image banks are speculative insofar as they materially develop entirely by the realities of their potential future production and exchange: casting a wide net of possible use values, photographers have to photograph object arrangements that are small and not too expensive but with large metaphorical potential that will hopefully do well, or "match" with semantics that for some reason are needed by the market. Beier's inquiry revealed that these are often absurd, slightly violent gestures—like a sinking bulb in water or a crab craw crushing a cigarette. The more extreme its semantic openness, the more an image will sell; its economy defines its poetry, and each

13
This methodology, while hardly aligned by any specific political discourse, echoes the ecological crisis of capitalist overproduction.

dialectically points to the other. These motifs are constantly reworked and reinvited by other photographers, for the chance of selling an image is greatest not when inventing a new motif but perfecting an existing one. In banks, such image clusters — some call them *territories* — spread quickly. Hundreds of variations exist on the theme "hammer and egg," for example.

With these nameless stock photographers, Beier shares the sculptural labor of producing semantic *potential* from what look like material "accidents," for these are not stable, immanent meanings. Rather, they arise if they are used — repurposed for *other* meanings. One would be surprised how many types of newspaper articles would find "hammer and egg" the most suitable artwork, yet in the image bank, their use value is dormant, still to be defined, and thus open. The logic behind Beier's return to material objects, to sculpture, can be found here: digital image production and circulation only accelerate processes that have long been at work in the world of material things, which are also constantly employed to *potentially mean something* in order to be rendered valuable and exchangeable but don't possess this meaning in any context, moment, or situation. Here returns Beier's dead dog: its ability to be and *be image* simultaneously, its status as worker and commodity, quite naturally embody the semantic dissonance or multivalence on which her work has since focused.

ANIMALS

Indeed, animals make frequent appearances in Beier's work. Consider *China* (2015), where decorative porcelain dogs (in a range of breeds) and porcelain vases (embellished, coincidentally, with animal scenes) were partially broken to reveal their hollow inside; *Beast* (2018), where mechanical rodeo bulls were retro-fitted with containers of infant formula; and *Empire* (2019), where a stack of Danish royal "China" porcelain plates fit neatly onto a vintage birdcage, producing an image of a dish rack. *Empire* framed the royal porcelain as caged birds, subliminally flipping the orientalism of Danish fairy-tale writer Hans Christian Andersen's *Nightingale* (1843) on its head while pointing to the materialist history of porcelain—that prized invention of China that European royal workshops spent centuries trying, and failing, to copy, until finally arriving at a successful knockoff sometime in the eighteenth century. In *China* and *Empire*, two types of porcelain objects oscillate between image, surface, and thing, retaining but a tenuous semiotic connection to "China" (the dog on display, for one, was manufactured in Italy); in *Beast*, "cow" implodes as a signified in the pull between nature, agriculture, industry, and entertainment, not at least because it may dawn on us that infant formula is a synthetic imitation of human breast milk while it is, in fact, materially based on commercial cow's milk, which itself, of course, is the result of the industrialization of one animal's milk intended for calves, that is to say, *their* babies (not ours). Beier's poetry of the animalesque goes on and on.

It was Donna J. Haraway, another intellectual animal lover, who, in her reading on Marx, summarized commodified animal lifeworlds as "value becoming flesh again, in spite of all the dematerializations and objectifications inherent in market valuation."[14] Haraway was writing about her dog, about which (or would she rather say whom?) she wrote an entire book. In it, Haraway muses that domesticated animals such as dogs are inversely uncanny (a term that, since Freud, has often been defined as the "not-quite-human") in that they are non-human "made-more-human" through our interaction with them — first by genetically modifying them into relative passivity by way of selective breeding, and secondly, to exchange with them through care, consumption, utility, or a combination of these. Dominance, power, and politics run through all these social modalities, as per Appadurai's dictum: a wrestling between being and thing, between nature, subject, and commodity. The animal puts up a mirror to an ongoing politics that mixes the symbolic, the affective, the social, the material-economic, and the cultural in a bewildering and often uncomfortable hodge-podge. Like Appadurai, I call these politics because they speak intensely to power struggles, not only between the living and the inanimate but between the material and the symbolic regimes under which both are destined to exist.

These sinister findings only crystalize in Beier's treatment of the human, who is not spared by the artist as a motif of labor and commodity relations. For just as the

14
Donna J. Haraway, *The Companion Species Manifesto: Dogs, People, and Significant Otherness*, edited by Matthew Begelke (Prickly Paradigm Press, 2003), 45.

dog labors in performance economies, so does the human—and also in the economy of contemporary art. Beier frequently works with artists and performers to respond to her sculptural environments, where they work as autonomous agents that navigate, use, activate, or find rest; this is the case in the artist's frequent collaborations with artist Bob Kil, such as *Life Guardians* (2022), where Kil led a group of performers to climb and simulate "riding" Beier's marble lions as a symbolic attempt of taming them. Others are directly representative of the task-based dimension of waged labor, such as in the recurring *The Pack* (2012), where she employs a mysteriously lone smoker to chain-smoke an entire pack of cigarettes outside the opening of her exhibitions, after which they are free to leave. In both cases, the human body is commodified as it labors for pay—the activities of the performers are dictated by the time they are remunerated to be there—but in the latter, the aesthetic representation (and, in turn, our conceptualization) of such labor is more complicated. We could say that the image of the lone smoker, propagated by media since the cowboy (think James Dean), is already in itself "valuable" in that it produces a certain sociocultural semantics—of nonchalant mystery, cool, and sexuality. But concretely, the value of the smoker's labor is now dictated by a product—namely, its standardized twenty-a-pack design. To make matters worse, this is a product that the smoker usually willingly *spends* money on (money, we can assume, the smoker has made through laboring for a wage—elsewhere). Dialectical vertigo ensues if one stays with *The Pack* too long: it may dawn on us, for example, that smoking outside a workplace (such as an art museum) would usually represent a "smoking break," that is, a temporary pause in production. How would the act of smoking qualify, in this case, then? The smoker, after all, is free to leave, fully remunerated, upon finishing his pack. Does it matter if they decide to inhale—will they smoke "for real" when they are done working?

THE PILE

My own entry to Beier's work was *Portrait Mode* (2011), realized a year before the aforementioned *Tragedy*: a towering triptych of framed clothing items in "exotic" animal prints, a biographical work of sorts, harking back to her childhood, which was partially spent in Mozambique, where *living* versions of such species exist quite uncontroversially. In an interview, Beier recalls frequently encountering these exotic prints in Mozambique's wastepile clothing markets, where the sartorial overproduction of fashion trends in the West goes to change hands or slowly decompose:

> When I lived in Mozambique, a load of donated clothes would arrive in our neighborhood every few months, and all the kids would run up and find sweatshirts from some Norwegian sports club, stone-washed jeans or a pair of leopard-print tights. The idea of leopard print arriving in a country where the leopard is a native animal from one where it's not—and all the financial and geopolitical agendas that are woven into the fabric along the way—fascinates me.[15]

Beier's artwork, whose formal composition recalls abstract expressionism, takes these mysterious issues of global capitalism—trend-making, commodity manufacturing, and object obsolescence—into the frame of art, commingling with the ontology of the painterly frame—not only as a commentary of art's reifying ability (that would be Duchamp) but as an attempt to reflect on the entire (opaque) life stories of generic products (which, yes, may eventually include being framed and *becoming an artwork*, at least since the time of Dada). The artwork's title suggests a portrait of a ubiquitous process that is hard to grasp and even harder to represent—the trendification of animals, that is to say, their *becoming-product* either *directly* (as fur) or *as image* (pattern).

Garment production, in particular, illuminates what Appadurai in the aforementioned text calls *commodity ecumene*: "transcultural networks of relationships linking producers, distributors, and consumers of a particular commodity or set of commodities."[16] The word *ecumene* historically connotes the "known," mappable part of the world, an acknowledgment of the limits of any epistemology of representation, as well as its implication in economization and political dominance through, for example, colonialism. "I guess I'm collecting these objects because they are the best and most

15
Kristian Vistrup Madsen, "How I Became an Artist: Nina Beier," *Art Basel*, April 30, 2024, accessed August 2024, https://www.artbasel.com/stories/how-i-became-an-artist-nina-beier-danish-letting-objects-speak-personal-theory-of-relativity-seeing-the-world-from-two-perspectives.

truthful witnesses and testaments to our world order," Beier has said about her objects. And she is right—but behind this statement lies a tragedy: that even through its things, the world remains, still, frustratingly unknowable.[17] Commodities may technically be products of their manufacturing, distribution, and exchange, but beyond the label indicating their country of manufacture, they are inherently inscrutable; they never fully reveal themselves. Therein lies our impulse, or compulsion, to render them symbolic, to *interpret* them so as to make them otherwise meaningful. For all its signifying potential, a printed fuchsia leopard T-shirt from H&M does not reveal its vast worlds; its ecumene, if you will, is enormously small, spanning only the last parts of its life as a purchased item (its journey from shop to closet). We know little of the soil where its cotton grew, the laboring hands that picked it, not to mention the origin of the chemical dyes, the source of the animal pattern, and so on. Were there animals involved in any of these processes? Here, the semiotics truly fail us. Beier, too, struggles with perceiving the total reality of the product form; her works are questions with only partial answers, posed to us as much as herself as an uncertain bricoleur. As a dialectical image of framed trash, *Portrait Mode* renders visible several gaps between signs and referents, between matter and symbol—setting its semiotic content ("animal") into profound existential limbo, first and foremost for the sculptor herself.

TYPES

If a Mozambiquan wastepile of European fast fashion is an accurate image for Beier's sculptural purview, the artist herself is rendered the ragpicker. Indeed, Beier is unafraid to admit that she's a hoarder. She collects widely: Chinese vases, giant seeds, money, underwear, marble eggs, Hermès ties, or dozens of mid-century pastel-colored sinks in particular undulating shapes.

If the ragpicker of the nineteenth century repurposed the debris of large cities at the cusp of industrialization, Beier's collecting points to the overwhelming sameness that pervades

16
Appadurai, 27.

17
Rasmus Kyllönen, "In the Studio: Nina Beier," *Collectors Agenda*, accessed August 2024, https://www.collectorsagenda.com/en/in-the-studio/nina-beier.

today's consumer culture; a world, one could say, of endless amounts of discarded marble countertops. It is this sameness, a culture of types and systems of objects, that first allowed Barthes and Baudrillard to develop their ambitious consumer semiotics some fifty years ago. And Beier's ability to accrue entire collections of object types is itself salient as material historical data, for it points to a concrete history of homogenization and standardization of manufacturing of consumer goods in the early twentieth century. As the commodity world exploded in variety and counterfeit ran wild, political, intellectual, and artistic forces in Western Europe came together to develop philosophies of "typification" (*Typierisierung*) meant to guide the consumer to well-designed, quality products. "Through mass production, an entirely new kind of commodity enters commerce, a species which did not exist before," wrote German architectural theorist Hermann Muthesius in 1917, subliminally conflating the world of animals with that of things.[18] The implication is clear enough, for industrial typification has produced a cultural perception of products belonging to "species" within which there are only minor variations, not unlike our idea of "leopard print" as it manifests across live animals, toys, and stockings.

Beier, we can safely assume, has long known as much. The artist always tries to collect as many versions of an object as possible, for as she once explained, it is somewhere in between the iterations—between the many typified images of "a sink"—that the "real object exists."[19] This relates not only to how manufacturing methods have shaped an object but also how cultures and economies have shaped it or changed it over time.

FINESSE

Beier's sinks—ubiquitous in Danish mid-century homes—were piling up in the artist's studio for years before they eventually became *Plug* (2018), where each sink's plug was retrofitted with a hand-rolled cigar. The cigar is a particularly semantically "heavy" product considering its dense symbolism of wealth and decadent pleasure, its direct manifestation

18
Hermann Muthesius, *Handarbeit und Massenerzeugnis*, 4, in Frederic J. Schwartz, *The Werkbund: Design Theory and Mass Culture before the First World War* (Yale University Press, 1996), 100.

19
Kyllönen.

of manual labor, its implication in mortality, and the history of slavery. If such associations would qualify as parts of the "life biography" of the cigar in the Appadurian sense, *Plug* delivers this with a fabulating sculptural finesse: by sticking it into the plug of a sink. Why? How is such a gesture justified by Beier, who could be mistaken (at least from reading this essay) as a hardcore conceptualist? Except, Beier's objects are intensely sensual, if not downright perverse (if in doubt, just consult her animated massage chair, *Manual Therapy*, 2016) – that is to say, full of unresolved desire. Beier channels this potent energy *sculpturally* and does so to invite new epistemological engagement that is not disconnected from a historical materialism. The accidental fornication between sink and cigar, for example, produces a perfectly bricolaged idea: that the color styles of the sinks – "Bahama beige," "Bali brown," "Indian ivory" – semiotically conjure vague imperialist fantasies while, literally, washing our hands clean. Together, the wonderfully voluptuous sinks and the embarrassingly phallic cigars create an allegory of ingestion and excretion, or modern gender roles and sexual exoticism, conjured by a few simple sculptural fixes, *a kind of sensual fiddling*.

Beier describes this work, this labor that I have called bricolage, as a kind of *listening*—an identifying of crossings of symbolic content and concrete form. "I wouldn't be able to streamline this method for the life of me—I have to wait until they *find* each other,"[20] she once explained to an interviewer. Beier's explanation of her methodology is always characteristically self-erasing, as if these objects had the ability to produce dialectics of their own. But Beier is not (just) a maker of readymade sculpture; like the first readymade artist Marcel Duchamp, her work cannot deny a quiet virtuosity. She works just as vividly in the tradition of Franz West, Rosemarie Trockel, Sarah Lucas, and Cady Noland, sculptors who, in a masterly fashion, show that the virtuosic intervention by the hand into everyday objects can invite a drastic reorientation of our perception of them. This alternative sculptural canon confirms Lévi-Strauss's bricolage—the "seeking-out and the imposition of a meaning upon the object"—as not only a creative human tactic but as one essential to the history of contemporary art.[21] When the crevices of a carved marble lion are filled with milk (filling

20
Kyllönen.

21
Lévi-Strauss, *The Savage Mind*, 2.

out the prior sculptor's spatial negative), when you realize that cigar tobacco is sold as "plug tobacco," something dialectically literally "falls into place" in that it holds the contradiction of the symbolic, the material, and the materialist in place; that is, only until it doesn't—until another biographical layer is added to an object or object type and meanings disintegrate into flux once more. Beier's product dialectics continue to mutate and implicate new material, cultural, and historical categories in their process—including the art object itself, that most special modern product that maintains, even today, a heightened symbolic potential. Indeed, it is on this potential that the entire historical tradition of art-making rests; that objects of art are implicitly, self-evidently, and permanently *meaningful.* Here, Beier's work offers a final, seductively controversial claim: that this potentiality is not so different from any other type of object, any other commodity. Rather, it is typological, close to mass-produced, and as telling as a pile of marble lions or sinks.

Nina Beier, *Ø (Island)*
June 1 – October 27, 2024

Art Center Gl. Holtegaard
Attemosevej 170, 2840 Holte, Denmark

This volume is published by Gl. Holtegaard with Bierke Verlag on the occasion of *Ø (Island)*.

Artistic Director/Curator of the exhibition:
Kit Leunbach
Producer: Vanessa Boni
Head Technician: Heine Thorhauge Mathiasen
Head of Communication: Nina Peitersen

Author: Jeppe Ugelvig
Editor: Vanessa Boni
Graphic Design: James Langdon
Photograph: David Stjernholm
Proofreading: Mark Soo/linguistic.services
Print: Spreedruck, Berlin

Bierke Verlag, Berlin
bierke.de
mail@bierke.de

ISBN 978-3-948546-21-2
Printed in Germany

ACKNOWLEDGMENTS

This project would not have been possible without the generous support of Aage og Johanne Louis-Hansens Fond, Augustinus Fonden, Knud Højgaards Fond, William Demant Fonden, Overretssagfører L. Zeuthens Mindelegat, and the Danish Arts Foundation.

DISTRIBUTION

Public Knowledge Books, UK/EU
publicknowledgebooks.com
diane@publicknowledgebooks.com

NBN, USA/CA
nbnbooks.com
customercare@nbnbooks.com

Les presses du réel, FR/B/L/CH
lespressesdureel.com
info@lespressesdureel.com

GVA Göttingen, GER
gva-verlage.de
rabe@gva-verlage.de

Bierke Verlag

gl Holtegaard